Wait Till It Gets

DARK

A KID'S GUIDE to Exploring the Night

ANITA SANCHEZ
& GEORGE STEELE

Illustrated by John Himmelman

muddy boots™

we jump in puddles

D0204238

we jump in puddles

An imprint of Globe Pequot

Distributed by NATIONAL BOOK NETWORK

Copyright © 2017 Anita Sanchez
Cover and interior design by Diana Nuhn

British Library Cataloguing in Publication Information Available
Library of Congress Cataloging-in-Publication Data Available

ISBN 978-1-63076-318-3 (hardcover)
ISBN 978-1-63076-319-0 (e-book)

♾ The paper used in this publication meets the minimum requirements of American National Standard for Information Sciences—Permanence of Paper for Printed Library Materials, ANSI/NISO Z39.48-1992.

CONTENTS

To Lola, and to all the kids
who have shared nature with us.

INTRODUCTION

Night. It's scary out there. Time to go inside or not...?

There's a dark and mysterious world waiting to be explored—and it's just outside your door. By day, it's as familiar to you as the back of your hand: the same old yard, street, and houses you see every day. But just wait till it gets dark!

What's Going On Out There?

People usually get up in the morning, eat meals and do stuff during the day, then sleep at night. But what if it was the other way around? Imagine waking up in the evening, having lunch at midnight, and climbing into bed as the sun rises. That's what nocturnal animals do. Instead of sundown being the end of the fun, dusk is the time when everything begins.

For these creatures, night is the world they live in. Under the comforting cloak of darkness, they can hide from predators, hunt dinner, find mates. But when it's pitch dark, how do they do what they have to do? How do they keep from bumping into trees or falling off a cliff?

Nocturnal animals experience the world differently than we do. They can talk with their noses, taste smells in the air, and see light in different ways. They can smell scents and hear sounds that we can't.

Humans have keen senses, too—we're just not used to using them. Like playing the piano or learning to kick a soccer ball, sensing the night takes practice! We might not have eyes exactly like an owl's, or a nose as sharp as a wolf's, but humans can see, smell, and hear in the dark much better than we realize.

So get ready to step into the darkness! Maybe it's not that scary after all. You'll challenge your senses to the max as you explore. Everything you see, hear, touch, smell, and even taste will be different than in daytime.

Because everything changes when the sun goes down.

CHAPTER 1

EYES LIKE AN OWL

What can you see when it gets dark? Nothing, right?

Wait a minute.

In just sixty seconds of darkness, your eyes change. Ever walk into a darkened movie theater? At first, you're almost blind. Slowly, objects start to appear out of the blackness, until you can find your friends and choose a seat. Your eyes adapt to the low level of light—just like an owl's eyes.

Hunting in the Dark

On a chilly, moonless night, a great horned owl perches on a branch. Hours of darkness pass as the owl waits motionless, silent. Suddenly the owl tenses as its huge golden eyes glimpse a tiny movement in the leaves on the forest floor: the twitch of a mouse's tail. Instantly, the owl takes

flight, wings and talons outstretched.

A great horned owl, hunting for its prey in a midnight forest, has the same problem you do in the theater—to find the way in low levels of light. An owl has to fly through a maze of trees, avoiding twigs, branches, rock, and other obstacles. With split-second timing, the owl targets a small rodent hidden in deep shadow.

Of course, an owl's face is covered with feathers while yours is covered with skin. But on the inside, your eyeballs work pretty much the same.

In both owls and humans, light enters the eyeball through

the pupil and then travels through the lens onto the retina. The retinas of both owls and humans are lined with millions of tiny cells that are sensitive to light, called *photoreceptor cells*. Some of these cells are shaped like a long, thin

You Can Do It:
Keep an Eye on Your Eye

Look into a mirror and check out your eye. The colored part—blue or brown or hazel—is called the iris. In the center of the iris is a shiny black dot called the pupil.

The pupil is like a window that allows light to enter the eye. Without you being aware of it, your pupils automatically get bigger in the dark to allow more light into your eyes. When there's a lot of light the pupils get smaller to protect the eyes.

Shine a flashlight at the mirror (don't shine the light directly into your eye). Quickly, your pupil becomes a tiny black dot. Once your pupil has shrunk, it takes a long time—more than half an hour—for it to open up again. You have to be in the dark for about 45 minutes for your night vision to be at the max.

ice cream cone and are called cone cells. Others are thin and stick-like, so they're called rods. Both rods and cones detect light and send a complex pattern of signals through

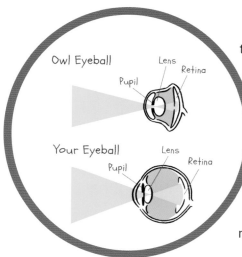

Owl Eyeball   Lens
                   Retina
        Pupil

Your Eyeball   Lens
                   Retina
        Pupil

the optic nerves to the brain.

Great horned owl eyes and human eyes are roughly the same size. But here's where human and owl eyes differ—we have more cones and they have more rods.

Colorful Cones

Cone cells let you see color, and they work best in daytime. They need a certain level of light to make them active, and if the light level sinks they can't do their job. (Remember COnes are for COlor.)

Black-and-White Rods

Rod cells need less light to function. They don't pick up color—they show the outlines of light and dark, in shades of black, white, and gray. Each of your eyeballs has about a hundred million rods. That seems like a lot, but owls have way more rods than humans do.

Rod cells are the best at detecting motion. An owl hunting at night doesn't need to see what color the prey is, so the owl doesn't need a lot of cones. Instead the owl uses the rod cells to spot the black shadow of a mouse moving among gray shadows of leaves.

It's Pitch Dark Out There—Or Is It?

Night is never totally dark. In fact, unless you're in a cave, it's all but impossible to find complete darkness outside.

A golden harvest moon can glow bright enough to read by. Even on nights of no moon—called the "dark of the

You Can Do It: Art in the Dark

Choose a few brightly colored crayons: blue, red, yellow, green. Then go outside when it's almost dark, with just enough light to see the paper and the crayons. Draw a picture: red house, blue sky, green grass, yellow sun. Sounds simple—but it's almost impossible!

In low-light levels you can see your hand moving across the page—that's your rod cells picking up movement. But your cone cells aren't getting enough light. At night, it's almost impossible to tell one color from another. When you bring the picture back inside, you might find you've drawn a green sky or red grass!

moon"—light sneaks in all around. The stars beam light from outer space. Electric lights from cities are reflected back to earth by clouds, and you can figure out the location of the nearest town by a glow on the horizon. And, unless you're deep in the wilderness, streetlights and headlights and windows are not far away—plenty of light to get your rod cells working.

Twice the Light

Another reason owls see in the dark better than humans is because owl eyes use light twice. A thin sheet of tissue, called the *tapetum lucidum*, carpets the back of an owl's retinas. Light goes into the eye, hits the rod cells, and then reflects off the tapetum lucidum like a sunbeam bouncing off a mirror. The light then hits the rod cells a second time on the way out.

You Can Do It: Flashlight Fun

When going outdoors at night, always take a flashlight for safety—and also for fun!

- Can you see the flashlight's beam? That means there's a lot of water in the air. In conditions of high humidity, like after a rainstorm or on a muggy night, the light bounces off tiny water droplets. You can brandish the long, glowing beam like a light saber.
- In low humidity—perhaps a cold, dry autumn night—the flashlight beam will be invisible until it touches something. Put your hand in the beam to watch it suddenly light up.
- Go outside on a rainy night, and light up the raindrops as they fall. Looks crazy!
- On a cool night, hold the flashlight in front of your face and watch what looks like smoke roll out of your mouth. The light is bouncing off tiny drops of water in your breath.
- Put the flashlight under your chin and shine it upwards to turn your face into a weird mask.

Other animals have eyes like this, too. Ever see a dog's eyes glow eerily green in a photograph? The eyeshine is caused by the reflected light from the dog's tapetum lucidum.

Humans will never see in the dark as well as an owl can. So for thousands of years, humans have created ways to beat back the darkness. No one knows how long ago

You Can Do It: The Disappearing Head

Stand in an area that's just light enough to see the outline of another person standing about fifteen feet away. Without moving your head (it's okay to blink), stare directly at the other person's head. Suddenly, their head will seem to fade away! As soon as you move your eyes, the head reappears. Be patient—when it finally works, it's awesome! Why does this happen?

By staring with the center of your eyes, you're aiming your cones directly at it—but in low light, the cones shut down. As they stop working, the object seems to disappear. As soon as you turn your head and move your gaze sideways, the rods are aimed at the object, and then you can see it again.

Could this be the origin of some of the ancient legends of headless horsemen and disappearing ghosts?

people first began to use tools to help them see in the dark torches, lamps, candles, and—most fun of all—on a night walk try to keep flashlights from shining directly into anyone's face. When a sudden beam of light hits the eyes, the pupils react instantly, snapping almost shut. That's why an owl flying across the road can be dazzled and confused by the headlights of an oncoming car. The pupils re-open much more slowly. So have fun with flashlights at the start of a night walk, then put them away for a while to let your night vision develop.

The Corner of Your Eye

Your rod cells are located mostly around the edges of the retina, while cone cells are clustered in the center. So in low-light levels, your peripheral, or side vision, works better. To observe a faint star, for example, glance at it sideways—looking out the corner of your eye.

You can't see in the dark as well as an owl can, but if you give your eyes enough time, you can see a lot more than you might think. So when you go outdoors at night, give the flashlight a rest, and let the night come slowly into focus.

And then, close your eyes and give your other senses a turn at being in charge! It's time to hear a little night music.

CHAPTER 2

EARS LIKE A FROG

Listen!

As the darkness deepens, we depend less on sight. So our other senses grow sharper. We become aware of sounds that were there all along—we just didn't notice them before. Turns out the night is filled with noises.

Leaves whisper. Wind sighs in the pine trees. Maybe an owl hoots, or a coyote yips. And in spring, ringing high over all the other sounds, you might hear a faint *peep-peep-peep*. Near forest ponds, meadow marshes, and puddles in the backyard, you can hear it rising out of the dark: the love song of the spring peepers.

What are spring peepers? They're tiny frogs, not much bigger than the tip of your thumb. And these little amphibians can make a huge noise.

Peepers hibernate, sleeping away the cold under logs or bark. In early spring they wake up, head for water, and begin to give their high, sweet call.

Night Singers

Why does the frog chorus tune up at night? Wouldn't it make more sense for frogs to go looking for each other in broad daylight?

You Can Do It: Big Ears

Make your external ears even bigger by cupping a hand behind (not over) each ear. Then listen carefully to the sounds of night. Every sound will be louder—it will seem as though someone has turned up the volume!

Sounds travel through the air in waves. The bigger your ears are, the better they can capture sound waves and funnel them to your ear drum.

With hands behind your ears, slowly turn around. Which is the noisiest direction? The quietest? Can you locate the direction of a nearby highway, or a tree with rustling leaves?

Unfortunately for frogs, they're a favorite menu item for a lot of predators. So if a frog doesn't want to end up as lunch, it's safer to sing noisy love songs under cover of darkness. And frogs don't need daylight to find each other. Even if it's pitch dark, they can hear the night chorus with their sharp ears.

Wait a minute—frogs have ears? Actually, they do. They just don't have ears that stick out from the head (external ears) like humans or dogs. Big floppy ears would slow frogs down while swimming. Frogs have a flat disk of skin behind each eye, called the *tympanum*, or ear drum.

Think about a how a drum is made—it's a thin covering stretched tightly over a round frame. The eardrum is a circle of thin skin on a ring of cartilage. Your eardrums are deep inside your head—frogs' eardrums are on the surface. But both frog and human ears work in similar ways.

Sound waves hit the surface of the ear drum, making it vibrate like the top of a drum. These vibrations move through your head, traveling the spiraling pathways of the inner ear. The vibrations stimulate the auditory nerves to send signals to the brain, which decodes these signals as sounds.

Where Are You, Exactly?

A female peeper can find another peeper on the darkest night, even if they start off half a mile apart. That's a long way for an inch-long frog to travel! Hopping along a few inches at a time, she tracks the sound until she locates the exact lily pad or blade of grass that the male is sitting on.

How does she do it? Frogs (and people) have two ears, of course, one on each side of the head. A frog's brain, like yours, automatically figures out that if sound hits one ear before the other, a bit more loudly, then that must be the direction the sound is coming from.

Actually, a frog's whole body is one big ear! They can feel sounds vibrating inside their mouths, in the lungs, and all through the body cavity. All this information helps them zero in on a sound's location.

What a Racket!

When a whole lot of frogs are singing together, they're loud enough to hurt your ears!

On a spring night, different species of frogs might be singing, water flowing, insects buzzing. And it's too dark to see anything! How do frogs find one another in all that noise?

You Can Do It: Ear-watching

Watch an animal that has external ears—a pet dog or cat, or maybe a rabbit or a deer—and observe how their ears move. If you make a sudden sound, they'll aim their ear in that direction. They might not bother to turn their head— they just swivel their flexible external ears to pinpoint sounds.

The female frog's ears are able to pick out just the right signals from this complex blend of sounds. They can identify a male of the same species, even in a pond full of thousands of other frogs. Scientists are still trying to figure out exactly how female frogs pull this off, and they've discovered that some types of frogs can close part of their ear tubes, like pulling a curtain across a window. This blocks out less important noises, especially lower-pitched sounds like water splashing, and lets the frog concentrate on the higher-pitched mating calls. Figuring out how frog ears can screen out some sounds and focus on others could help people create "intelligent" hearing aids for humans—hearing aids that can ignore background traffic noise and home in on the human voice.

Creak, Quack, and Plunk

There are lots of different kinds of frogs, and it can be hard

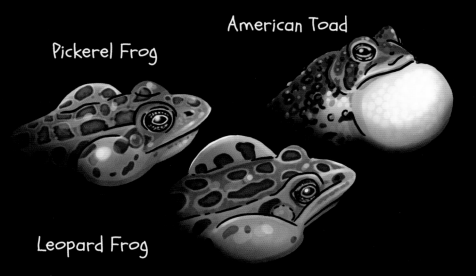

American Toad

Pickerel Frog

Leopard Frog

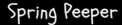
Spring Peeper

even for *herpetologists* (scientists who study reptiles and amphibians) to tell them apart. For example, leopard frogs look very much like pickerel frogs. But each species has its own special call: leopard frogs creak like a rusty hinge, pickerel frogs sound like a person snoring. Even in the dark, the female frog can't mistake one for another.

There's a whole symphony of frog songs, and these musical amphibians keep up the concert all through the spring. Wood frogs join in, sounding exactly like ducks quacking. Then green frogs go "plunk!" like a banjo string, while American toads sing a high-pitched trill. Late in the spring, bullfrogs shout "jug-o-rum" in deep voices.

Bullfrog

Wood Frog

Green Frog

You Can Do It: Hide-and-Listen!

Find a park, playground, or any outdoor area where you can safely go at night. Invite a few friends to a game of hide-and-listen.

Give each person a different kind of noisemaker. (Don't use a really loud one, like a whistle—invent something quieter, like crinkling paper, or blowing over the top of a soda bottle.) Hiders should hide behind trees, bushes, slides, or see-saws while the seeker counts to twenty without looking. It's dark, so the hiders don't have to go far.

Once everyone is hidden, the seeker claps once—and everyone has to answer with their sound. The seeker uses "big ears" to track their calls. Repeat until everyone is discovered.

When you're the seeker, did using the "big ears" technique help you find the callers?

Go Frogging!

On a spring night, take a flashlight, and head outside to any place that's wet. A mother frog doesn't necessarily need a big swamp or pond for her eggs. Many frogs mate in temporary *vernal pools*—shallow hollows in the ground that fill up with water in the spring rains, and then dry up in summer's heat. Some frogs will even lay eggs in mud puddles or on swimming pool covers.

Listen carefully, using your "big ears." If you hear frogs calling, move closer—but be quiet. If the frogs hear you coming, they'll clam up! Shine a flashlight over the surface of the water. You may see tiny sparkles of eyeshine—the tapetum lucidum of a frog reflecting light back at you.

It's not just frogs who are making noise at night.

On a night walk, how many nocturnal sounds can your "big ears" catch?

Once spring nights warm up, you'll hear the earliest cricket chirps, then katydids chime in, telling mates

You Can Do It: Help the Hoppers!

Sometimes frogs have to travel long distances to water—and if their path crosses a road, they don't know they have to look both ways! When you're in the car on a spring night, be on the lookout for frogs crossing roads, and warn drivers to slow down.

Here I am! Raccoons yowl and yelp as they fight over a tipped garbage can. Owls hoot in a special pattern to warn rivals: *Go away!* Humans use sound for night-time communication, too—sirens, car horns, and ringtones say *Look out!* or *Come here!* The night air is filled with conversations.

Listen!

True
Katydid

CHAPTER 3

A NOSE LIKE A DEER

The deer are rustling shadows as they glide through night-time forests, meadows, and your backyard. White-tailed deer can make sounds, of course, and they snort or grunt once in a while. But usually, they talk with their noses. Deer have most of their conversations by using their sense of smell.

A deer's nose is huge compared to a human nose, even though deer are approximately human-size. Inside a deer's big nasal cavity is plenty of room for more than a hundred million *olfactory* receptor cells, which carry information from the nose to the brain with lightning speed.

White-tailed deer constantly use their noses to find out what's going on around them, and to share information with each other. They can create a whole vocabulary of scents with small organs called *glands*. Scattered over a deer's

You Can Do It: Learning with Your Nose

Usually, we don't notice smells much, unless they're really good, or really bad. You might wonder—why do I even need a sense of smell? Wouldn't it be better not to smell that dirty diaper or stinky garbage?

Human noses might not have as many scent receptor cells as other mammals do, but we definitely get a lot of information from smells. It takes practice to learn to listen to the "voice" of your nose telling you what's going on.

The warm scent of popcorn says a movie theater is around the corner. Fresh, salty air means the sea is nearby. A funny smell from a turkey sandwich warns that the meat is going bad—better not take a bite!

Close your eyes and sniff—what can you smell right now?

body, from head to toe, each gland oozes a liquid that has a different type of smell. And each smell, to the sensitive nose of a deer, has a different meaning.

When a buck (male deer) rubs his head against a branch, a strong scent from a gland on his forehead is left behind. Other bucks can detect the smell, even days later. A "buck rub" is the deer's way of shouting: *This is my territory!*

Deer also have scent glands on each foot, wedged

Scent gland
beneath deer hoof

between the two sections of their hoof. Every step a deer takes leaves a smell on the ground, a scent unique to that particular deer—as individual as a fingerprint for a human. Another deer, sniffing the trail, can tell if a family member passed by. Since the smell changes over time, the sniffer can also learn how long ago the trail was made. A fawn can easily find Mom just by sniffing her footprints, even if dozens of other deer have passed by. (Imagine if you could do that in a crowded shopping mall!)

You Can Do It: Tracking the Onion

Could you follow an invisible trail? Get together with some friends and track something smelly—like an onion!

Onions have a strong scent that lasts a long time—like the smell from a deer's scent glands. Take an onion half and rub the smelly juice on branches, benches, or rocks. Make each rub about two feet away from the last one. Challenge your friends to sniff their way along the trail, too. Ask someone else to leave an onion trail, then try tracking it yourself.

Stamping Out a Message

At dusk, a solitary doe stands on a hilltop, sniffing the scents drifting over the meadow. Suddenly, she smells a threat—a pack of dogs running toward her. Before turning to flee, she takes a moment to stamp a foot on the ground.

Why stamp? Slamming the hoof down leaves a lot of scent on the earth. Other deer following the same path later are warned to be on the alert: danger might lurk nearby!

Scent Molecules

Anything smelly—whether it's a flower, a freshly baked cookie, or an angry skunk—gives off chemicals that evaporate, molecule by molecule, into the air. You have to breathe in these tiny odor particles to smell them—you can't smell anything if you hold your breath. That's why dogs sniff so enthusiastically at a fire hydrant or garbage can—they're pulling scent particles into their noses. If you could get close enough to a deer investigating a buck rub, you might hear it sniffing like a bloodhound.

Humans are better smellers than we realize. Could you tell your own family members apart at night—just by sniffing them? It may seem impossible, but that's partly because we don't pay attention to what our noses are noticing.

Helen Keller, blind and deaf almost from birth, relied on smell to make sense of her dark world. She could tell one variety of rose from another, and even recognize individual humans—just by smelling them.

You Can Do It: Sharpen Your Nose

Put half a dozen strong-smelling things in separate brown paper bags: a slice of lemon, a pickle, cinnamon, an old sock. Mix the bags up. Then test yourself—can you identify the objects by nose alone?

Then make the test harder: Helen Keller could tell an orange from a tangerine by smell. Can you?

If you have pets, they probably sniff you a lot. Return the favor and sniff them—could you tell them apart by smell?

Outdoors, crumple up leaves to release their scents. Do dandelion leaves smell different from clover or grass? Breathe in the scent of a spicy pine cone or a cluster of spruce needles.

Get your nose right up close! The closer you are, the more you'll smell. On all fours, sniff dried leaves, the soil in a garden, or the bark of a tree.

News Carried on the Wind

Air surrounds us every minute of our lives. We usually don't notice air unless there's a strong wind howling. But air is continually flowing over the earth, surrounding us like an ocean of invisible water.

Indoors, air is quiet and unmoving, like a swimming pool. Going outdoors is like jumping into a turbulent river. Air moves over, under, and around us. It swirls around obstacles like walls or houses, ripples through the grass, and flutters leaves. And every night breeze carries a bewildering variety of scents.

We may not care which way the wind is blowing, but wind direction can be a matter of life and death to a deer. Every breath a deer takes is like reading a newspaper filled with information. *Humans approaching—that way! Coyote coming—this way. Mom's over there!*

You Can Do It: Which Way Is the Air Flow?

In an open spot, try to figure out the movement of air. Close your eyes and point your nose into the wind. Sometimes it seems as if there is no wind at all, so take a handful of something light, like dried grass, and let it fall to show which way the air is moving. Or blow bubbles and see which way they drift.

During hot summer days, sun-warmed air rises. As the temperature drops in the evening, cooling air masses sink and even slide downhill. At night, if you stand on a slope, you can often feel cool air rolling past you down the hill.

White-tailed deer are *crepuscular*, which means they're most active in times of low light: dawn and dusk. During the day, and in the middle of the night, they're less likely to be moving around—they spend a lot of time curled up in a bed of soft grass, sleeping or grooming themselves. Deer like a bedding spot near the top of a hill, with their backs to the wind. That way they can watch the slope in front of them, while sniffing for danger from behind. Ever wish you had eyes in the back of your head? Deer don't need them! It's tough to sneak up behind a deer, as long as the wind's in the right direction.

You Can Do It: Smell the Night

On a night walk, be aware of what your nose is telling you. Is there a sweet scent in the air—maybe a garden? Can you sniff out the location of the nearest water—the ocean, a marsh, or a pond? Is there campfire smoke in the air?

Figure out the clues the night breeze is bringing you. Can you smell car exhaust? That means there's a highway not far away. Or is there anything tasty nearby—can you follow your nose to a pizza restaurant or cotton candy stand?

Breathe Deep!

Usually we take tiny, polite breaths with our noses. But to really gather in scent molecules, you need to breathe deep!

You can inhale about a cupful of scent-laden air with each powerful sniff. Blow the air out with a grunt, and snort in some more!

   Point your nose into the wind and let the night air wash over you, carrying all its odors. What news is the night bringing you?

CHAPTER 4

A TONGUE LIKE A GILA MONSTER

Morning sun hits the desert like a hammer. The temperature shoots up fast. By afternoon, sand and rock can heat up to a hundred and fifty degrees. Any reptile crawling around would fry like an egg. So it's the cool of the night, after the sun goes down, when the monsters come out of their caves.

Like most desert dwellers, Gila (HEE-la) monsters wait out the heat. The big orange-and-black reptiles peer out from their underground burrows, then crawl slowly through the gathering darkness, searching for prey.

Gila monsters don't go hunting very often. In fact, they spend about ninety percent of their lives underground.

When the monsters hunt, they aren't seeking humans to devour. They only eat small prey, like baby rodents or the eggs or young of ground-nesting birds. One nest of quail eggs can last these slow-moving reptiles for months. You eat three meals a day, but a Gila monster might eat three meals a year!

On a moonless desert night, pitch-dark, how can a hungry monster find a tasty dinner? And how to avoid becoming food for a hunting coyote?

Gila monsters have tiny eyes, but they can see pretty well, and have good hearing. Like most nocturnal animals, they have a strong sense of smell. But something else is going on, too. They're also relying on their tongues for information. The long, thin tongue constantly flickers in and out as a Gila monster tastes the night.

You Can Do It: Help the Gilas

If you ever happen to see a Gila monster in the desert dusk, appreciate your good luck! Gila monsters are beautiful, and increasingly rare—in fact, they're an endangered species and it's illegal to harm or bother them. If you're in a car on a desert road, help the Gilas by watching out for them crossing roadways. Cars are by far their most dangerous predators.

What Does Darkness Taste Like?

Gila monsters taste things differently from the way you taste a cookie. The sensitive tongue picks up scent molecules from the night air with every flick. Then the lizard pulls the tongue back in, and sticks the forked tongue into two tiny holes on the roof of the mouth, like plugging an electrical plug into a socket.

The twin holes aren't nostrils, and they're not connected to the nose. They lead to a special organ, called the *vomeronasal organ* (VNO, also called Jacobsen's organ, after one of the scientists who discovered it). The VNO is like a tiny chemical-analyzing laboratory inside the reptile's head. It identifies each chemical signal and sends messages direct to the brain: *Food this way! Danger that way!*

The VNO seems like a second nose, but actually this sense is neither taste nor smell but something in between. Vomeronasal nerves don't connect to the same part of the brain as the olfactory nerves of the nose. The VNO recognizes subtle scents, picking up different molecules, ones that the nose doesn't notice.

Taste buds

Human Tongues Do It Differently

Look at your tongue in a mirror. On its surface are clusters of sensitive cells called taste buds. Human tongues might not be as graceful as a reptile's, and we can't flick them in and out as quickly, but taste is something we're really good at!

We work hard on taste—perhaps more than we do on any other sense. Think about taking a bite of something really good: you roll it on your tongue, think about it, compare it to another flavor—and make a point of remembering it. Humans have a highly developed sense of taste: we can effortlessly tell the difference between sweet, sour, salty, bitter, and can identify hundreds of different flavors.

Reptiles have very few taste buds, and usually not on their tongues—mostly scattered in the back of the throat, perhaps to warn them if they're about to swallow some-thing harmful. They don't taste things for pleasure the same way we do—or do they? No one knows for sure what things taste like to a Gila monster!

Smelling With Your Tongue?

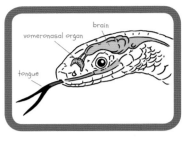

It's not only Gila monsters that smell with their tongues. Most reptiles have VNOs—that's why snakes are always flickering their tongues in and out. Lots of mammals have VNOs, too, including cats, cows, and mice. They open their mouths and lift their upper lips to expose the VNO to the air. (You might have seen a cat do this when checking out a new brand of cat food.) Elephants use the "finger" on the tips of their trunks to carry smells to their VNOs.

Do humans have the same ability to taste smells in the air? The answer is—no one knows!

This question is hotly debated by scientists. Human infants are born with the beginnings of a vomeronasal organ inside their mouths, but human VNOs don't seem to develop receptor cells as the baby grows. Some scientists argue that it's possible that human VNOs have different types of receptors that we haven't identified yet, and the VNO could still be transmitting messages to the brain. We just don't know.

The vomeronasal organ connects to the *amygdala*, a part of the brain that processes emotions. Perhaps at night, when our sense of sight is closing down, we pick up traces of scent molecules with our tongues without realizing it. Could it be that some of the emotions we feel so strongly in the dark—fear, joy, or love—are triggered by scents we detect as we taste the night-time?

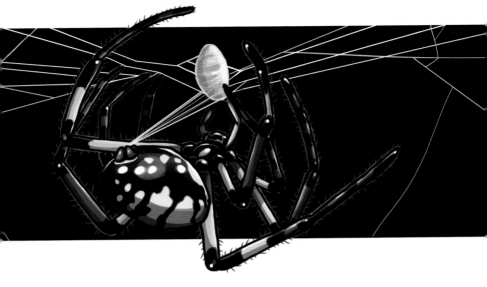

CHAPTER 5

FINGERS LIKE A SPIDER

You wake up blinking in the middle of the middle of the night. It's pitch dark, but you need to make a quick trip to the bathroom. Getting out of bed, yawning, you head down the hall, eyes half-closed.

No need for a light in this familiar territory—you just reach out to find your way. Your hand touches the smooth wall. Your toes tell you when you leave the carpeted hallway and step onto the chilly tiled floor.

Wait a minute! Turns out you're not the only one in the bathroom. What's that up in the corner—a little black blob in the middle of a web?

Spiders in the Dark

Spiders don't really have fingers, but they feel their way around the night. They have an incredible sense of touch. That's lucky for them, because their sight and hearing don't work so well.

Spiders do have eyes—most spiders have eight, in fact. Although they can see light and darkness and detect close-up movement, they can't see well far away. To a spider, you're just a big blob. And spiders don't have ears, so they can't hear you walking around. But a spider can feel the vibrations of your footsteps, and the currents of air you breathe out.

You Can Do It: Feel With Your Feet

The sole of your foot is very sensitive—that's why it's so ticklish! When walking in the dark, use your feet instead of your eyes to find your way.

Keep your weight on your back leg, and with the other, probe the ground in front of you. Bare feet can feel every tiny bump and pebble on the earth. Even with shoes on, you can feel if the surface you're walking on is gooey mud, bristly grass, or soft sand. Try walking at night in different shoes—slippers, sneakers, heavy boots. The thinner the sole, the more information you can gather.

Web Fingers

Web-spinning spiders have to avoid becoming someone else's food, so they usually wait till dark to begin creating a web. First they spin support threads to anchor the web in place. Then the supports are linked together with strands of sticky webbing. As the sun comes up, the trap is ready!

Motionless, the spider waits, holding onto thin lines of silk. The slightest jiggle of the web means: *Time for dinner!*

But what if it's a false alarm? Perhaps a leaf or a twig falls into the threads. Or what if the web traps a dangerous enemy—a wasp, perhaps—that could end up killing the spider? The web lines work as an extension of the spider's senses, like long stringy fingers. Each different twitch or pull reveals exactly what's going on in the web.

Sometimes, a jiggle might signal another spider—a male looking for a mate. The male shakes the web in just the right way so that the female knows not to rush out and eat him for dinner.

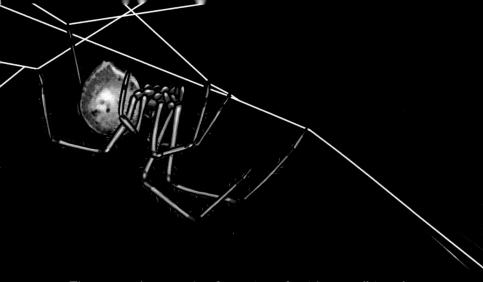

There are thousands of species of spiders stalking the night. Big black-and-yellow orb-weavers spin round webs in the garden. Funnel spiders make funnel-shaped webs in lawns and bushes. Jumping spiders don't spin webs, they leap onto their prey. Some spiders even hunt prey underwater!

You Can Do It: Check Out a Web

Can you find a spider's web? Almost any building will have webs in corners, draped over doorways, and tucked under windowsills. Check out outdoor lights—night-flying insects are attracted to lights, so the spider has a good chance of netting a tasty meal. Look up into the branches of trees, or low in the grass—webs are in all sorts of places.

Touch the webbing gently, using a twig or blade of grass. Which strands are sticky? The special threads for trapping prey will cling to your twig like glue. If it's an active web, the spider might venture out a little way to check you out, but it will quickly retreat. Be very careful not to destroy the web—it probably took the spider all night to make it!

Feeling All Over

Spiders don't only use their legs to feel things. Their whole bodies are constantly sensing the night's touch.

We have soft skin on the outside, and the hard bones that support our bodies are inside. A spider's body is protected with a hard outer covering called an *exoskeleton*. You'd think that wearing your skeleton on the outside would armor you against feeling anything, but a spider's exoskeleton isn't a solid shell. It has thousands of tiny areas called *sensilla slits*. The slightest pressure on these slits warns the spider: *Something's coming!*

A hairy spider can give you the creeps! But the hairs on a spider's body are acting as its nose, tongue, and fingers. Spiders smell and taste things with chemically sensitive hairs on their legs. And many of those scary bristles are *tactile* hairs, with nerves sensitive to the slightest touch. Even the breeze from the insect's wings bends the spider's tactile hairs a tiny bit, and tells the spider: *Dinner getting closer!*

Sensitive Skin

Like spiders, we can sense the night with our whole bodies. Fingertips are what you usually use for touching, but in every square inch of human skin, there can be a thousand or more nerve endings. Like long pieces of string, nerves wind through your body, up your spinal cord, to your brain. When you touch something, a complex blend of chemical and electrical signals is sent flashing in a split second to your brain. *Hot! Freezing! Prickly, fluffy, raspy, slippery!* Messages are constantly flowing from all over your skin to your brain.

Not much can hide from a spider's senses. So that spider in the bathroom knows you're there! But she won't bother you—you're way too big to eat! She'll just sit in a corner of the web—maybe even help you out by capturing some mosquitoes, or a fly or two. So don't bother the spider, and she won't bother you! Just turn out the light and feel your way back to bed.

You Can Do It: Touch the Night

Night is the best time to practice your sense of touch. Reach out and feel the texture of the human-made world: a rough brick wall, or a cold, smooth metal sign.

Then explore the textures of nature. Bend down and feel shaggy grass or velvety moss. Touch the cool, chalky bark of a white birch—it's totally different from the craggy bark of an oak or maple.

Remember it's not just about fingers! Brush your cheek against the delicate petals of a flower. When you sit on the ground, be aware of the coolness of earth beneath you. Feel the night with your whole body—just like a spider.

You Can Do It: Night Scavenger Hunt

Don't collect things—just touch them.
Can you find something:

-Sticky
-Fuzzy
-Papery
-Bumpy
-Damp
-Warm
-Feathery
And what else?

CHAPTER 6

FEET LIKE A FOX

On a cold winter morning, early sunlight reveals a fresh string of tracks in the snow. Little round paw prints, one after the other like a row of dots. Who was prowling the winter night? These tracks say clearly: *a fox was here!*

Red foxes are experts at combining all their senses to navigate the night. Of course, animals don't use their senses one at a time, like switching channels on TV. A hunting fox sniffs the night air as long, delicate paws feel the ground. Big ears are alert for sounds of a mouse rustling or a rabbit nibbling, while keen eyes catch every tell-tale movement. The fox begins the night's hunt, using all the clues the senses have to offer.

Where Are the Foxes?

Foxes in your neighborhood—no way, right? But it's very likely foxes are denning not far from where you are right now, even if you live in a city. Foxes live all over the United States—but they're seldom seen.

Although foxes are in the same family as wolves and coyotes, they're much smaller. A full-grown red fox weighs not much more than a large house cat. And they're very good at hiding, even in little patches of brush and clumps of trees.

Time for Dinner

What do foxes eat? The answer is—almost anything! Like dogs, foxes aren't picky eaters—
they're *omnivores*

who eat all kinds of stuff. Foxes love juicy berries. If they found a dropped peanut butter sandwich, they'd eat that, too. In summer, they catch beetles and crickets, but especially in winter, small mammals like rabbits and mice are foxes' main food.

To sneak up on a wary mouse or a big-eared rabbit, you have to be quiet! By moving slowly and choosing where to place each paw, foxes can move through the night in almost total silence.

Can you?

You Can Do It: Silent Walking

At night, walk across an open space like a lawn, being aware of every sound you make. Not just your foot-steps, but your breathing, the crunching of grass blades, and even your sleeve brushing against your coat.

Now try walking without making a single sound. Breathe slowly. Hold your arms out to the side so they won't rub against your jacket. Make sure your pant legs don't brush against each other.

Try different surfaces. Walking silently on a sidewalk is surprisingly hard. Hint: start each step from the outside, then roll your foot to the center. Then try a lawn.

Finally, you're ready for the biggest challenge of all—fox—walking through a night-time forest.

Foxes can't swoop through the air like owls can—they have to stalk their prey over crunchy dried leaves and dead sticks waiting to snap. So how do foxes and other hunters manage to move so quietly? One careful step at a time.

A stalking predator might take one step per minute. Think about that—one step per *minute*. That requires a lot of patience—and very good balance.

You Can Do It: How Slow Can You Go?

You can move much more quietly if you slow down. While walking outdoors at night, try moving in super-slow motion. Can you take a step that lasts an entire minute? (Set a stopwatch to time yourself—a minute can be a looooong time!)

Foxes have one big advantage over humans—with four feet, it's easier to balance.

Foxes use the same pathways again and again. It's energy-efficient, and can also save their lives! Following a familiar path helps them escape if they're being chased by a dog or coyote. The fox knows the path even in the dark, but the pursuer doesn't. Mother foxes show the routes to their young, and so a trail may be used by generations of wily foxes.

You Can Do It: Go On a Track Hunt

On a snowy night, take a flashlight and go hunting for fox tracks. Check under hedges, along fence lines, and the edges of yards to see who's been prowling.

You'll know you've found fox sign if you find a row of oval tracks slightly bigger than a cat's. Fox tracks are all in a row, because foxes use a pattern of movement called perfect stepping. They place their hind foot in the same place that the front foot stepped. This uses far less energy, especially in deep snow.

Maybe you'll come across other tracks: deer, rabbits, or squirrels. Look for your own tracks, too!

You might never see more of wary foxes than their tracks, but your other senses might pick up clues that they're not far. Listen for a high-pitched yip as one fox calls to another at the start of a night's hunting. Or you might sniff the faint skunky odor of a fox's hidden den. Whether or not you see them, the foxes are out there, exploring the winter night, walking silently along their age-old trails.

Fox

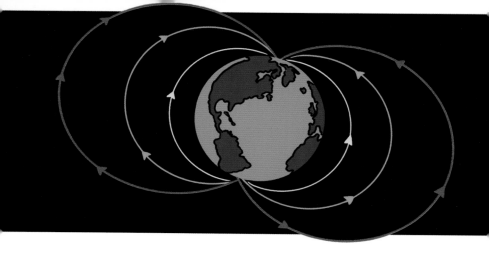

CHAPTER 7

THE MYSTERIOUS SIXTH SENSE

Sight, hearing, smell, taste, and touch—they're your tools to explore the night. But what if there are other senses—ones we don't even realize we have?

A Living Compass

On a spring night, you might hear the cheerful "hink-honk" of migrating geese, returning to their nesting grounds after a winter down south. On a moonless, cloudy night, how do they find their way? Whales swimming in the blackness of the ocean deeps know which way to go to their summer feeding grounds. Even tiny snails orient themselves at night without using stars or the moon as a guide. How do they do it? Homing pigeons are famous for their uncanny ability to find their way home over immense distances, and for centuries people wondered how the birds managed it. Experiments showed that it wasn't only the sun, stars,

You Can Do It: Head North!

There's nothing more bewildering than trying to find your way in darkness. As night falls, landmarks become hard to see. Bright red or yellow trail markers fade to gray. In the dark it's harder to keep walking straight, and it's all too easy to veer off course. Learning how to use a compass can keep you pointed in the right direction. (Be sure to remember your flashlight so you can read the compass in the dark!)

To use a compass, hold it flat. The red tip of the needle will point to Earth's North Magnetic Pole, so when you follow the needle you are heading north. East is to your right, west is left. South is behind you.

What landmarks are to the north of your house? Can you see skyscrapers, mountains, or the glow of a city in the distance? On a clear night, you can see the northern constellations, including stars in the Big Dipper, and the North Star. All these directional clues can help you find your way home.

north star ·

little dipper

big dipper

or landmarks that guided the birds. No matter how black the night, they could find their way. Then researchers discovered that attaching tiny magnets to the birds' feathers totally threw off their ability to return home. The birds were guided by a powerful—but invisible—current of magnetism that flows around the earth from pole to pole.

Our planet's core is mostly molten iron, and the spinning of the earth turns it into a big magnet. The magnetic field extends out into space for thousands of miles, surrounding the whole planet.

If an animal is going somewhere in the dark—whether it's hundreds of miles or just up and down a leaf—it's a big

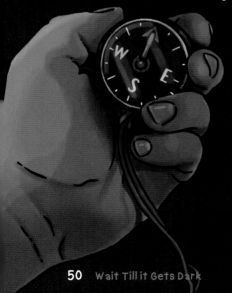

advantage to have a built-in GPS! Migrating birds, dolphins, beetles, lobsters, sea turtles, even bacteria—all sorts of creatures use the earth's magnetic field to find direction.

Heading North

People can navigate by the earth's magnetic field, too, but we need tools to help us. A compass has a magnetized needle that points north, no matter which way you turn. Seems like magic—there's an invisible force moving that needle! You can't see it, or smell it, taste, touch, or hear it. But the compass proves that Earth's magnetic field is constantly flowwing all around you.

Pounce!

In a winter forest, a wildlife biologist studying fox behavior watched dozens of foxes hunting mice. While patiently videotaping more than six hundred pounces, he noticed something weird. Even when the foxes couldn't see their prey under the snow, the foxes were more than three times as successful when they pounced north. Jumping in any other direction, their prey was much more likely to escape. Could it be, he wondered, that the foxes were sensing the pull of the earth's magnetic field, and using it to help their hunt?

But how could a fox figure out exactly which way is north? Scientists are still trying to solve this mystery. A lot of the research on magnetic sensing has involved birds, and biologists have discovered that pigeons and some other birds have particles of magnetite, a magnetic mineral, embedded in their beaks. Other birds have *cryptochromes*, special types of proteins in the cone cells of their eyes, which react to magnets, and may help birds actually see the Earth's magnetic field as a pattern of dark shapes. But so far no one knows exactly how some creatures turn themselves into living magnets.

A Seventh Sense?

Could humans possibly have this sense, too? There are some tantalizing hints that humans may be able to tap into the earth's magnetic field. Scientists have recently discovered cryptochromes in the retinas of human eyes. Imagine if someday we could learn to see the magnetic field as it flows along the earth's axis. We could be our own GPS, using our eyes as living compasses.

We're only beginning to unlock the possibilities of the sense of magnetoreception. Are there perhaps other untapped senses hidden inside us? Perhaps you'll be the scientist to discover the mysterious seventh sense!

Night. It's dark out there, yes—but not scary. Time to go outside!

Flip off the porch lights, put your flashlight in your back pocket, and head outdoors. Fox-walk softly as you sniff and savor the night air. Let your pupils open wide to capture every bit of light. As the blackness starts to reveal shapes and shadows, use your "big ears" to scoop up the night's secret sounds.

Congratulations! You've metamorphosed into a nocturnal animal.

east

north

south

You Can Do It: Compass Directions

It takes practice to use a compass with accuracy. Try following a compass on this mini-treasure hunt:

Take 15 steps north.

Now, turn to the right and take 15 steps east.

Then go in the opposite direction from the way the needle is pointing: 15 steps south.

Last, face north again, then turn and walk 15 steps to the left, which is west.

If you're reading the compass properly, you should end exactly where you began.

X

We Need the Dark

Darkness is in danger!

Humans have done such a thorough job of lighting up the night that real darkness has become hard to find. We tend to think of light as "good" and darkness as "bad," but too much light can destroy the beauty and mystery of the nighttime. Without darkness we can't see the Milky Way, or wish on a falling star. We need night so we can listen to katydids and coyotes, watch bats swoop and dart, and enjoy firefly fireworks.

Wildlife need the night, too. "Light pollution" can harm animals as much as toxic chemicals do. Countless species need natural cycles of light and dark to migrate, hunt for food, and find mates. Even plants depend on light cues for growing and making seeds. When we light up the night, we lose the natural rhythm of light and dark.

Save the Dark

A lightbulb is not always a bright idea! Much of the artificial lighting that humans use is wasted in uselessly lighting up the sky. Take a look at the outdoor lighting in your yard and neighborhood. Is there a way it could be more dark-sky friendly?

🦇 Could your family use dimmer switches, timers, or motion sensors to cut down on outdoor lighting?

🦇 Turn off lights, especially outdoor lights, when not in use (a great way to save energy and money, too.)

🐾 For information on dark-sky friendly lighting, see the website of the International Dark-Sky Association: http://darksky.org/lighting/lighting-basics/

Find the Dark

Where can you go to explore nature at night? Your own back-yard is the first place to start. Are there parks or playgrounds in your neighborhood that you can safely visit at night?

Then check out your local nature center or community park—do they offer night programs like owl prowls or night-time nature walks? A bird club might have guided walks to seek out nocturnal birds like woodcock, whip-poor-wills, and owls.

Also, look for local astronomy clubs—many organizations of astronomers hold "star parties" and welcome amateur stargazers. They know where the darkest places are!

The International Dark Sky Foundation is an organization that works to protect nature's darkness. They designate places, including state and national parks, as Dark Sky Preserves. Find out if there's one near you at http://darksky.org.

Counting in the Dark

To help nocturnal animals, scientists need to know more about them: where they're found, when they're most active, how many there are. How do you count all the frogs or fire-flies in North America? By getting a lot of people to help!

Every year, people all over the world go outdoors to watch and listen to nocturnal animals. They report their findings to on line databases that help keep track of wildlife populations. Here's a sampling of possible Citizen Science programs—there are many others!

🦟 Want to help keep the frog chorus singing? Check out FrogWatch USA, a program of the Association of Zoos and Aquariums. https://www.aza.org/become-a-frogwatch-volunteer

🦟 Do you love to watch fireflies sparkling at night? Clemson University sponsors the Vanishing Firefly Project. They offer a mobile app that helps to measure firefly populations in parks and backyards. http://www.clemson.edu/public/baruch/firefly_project/

🦟 Celebrate National Moth Week! Every year, during the last week in July, "moth-ers" of all ages observe and document moths in their backyards and neighborhoods. See the website of the American Entomological Society. https://entomologytoday.org

Be Safe in the Dark

Always carry a flashlight at night, even if you don't plan to use it. 🦟 If you're planning a long night hike, scout out the terrain in daytime first. Be aware that as night falls, things look different—trail markers and landmarks can be harder to find.

🦟 Make sure someone knows where you're going and when you expect to be back.

Adaptation – a feature or characteristic of an organism that helps it survive.

Cartilage – connective tissue in animal bodies that is stiff but not as hard as bone. It is an important part of the skeleton, making up parts of the nose and ears.

Crepuscular – having to do with the time just before the sunrise and just after the sun sets. Crepuscular animals are most active at dawn and dusk.

Diurnal – having to do with day. Diurnal animals are most active during the day and spend the night quietly in sheltered places.

Exoskeleton – the hard protective covering of animals that do not have an internal bone skeleton.

Herpetologist – a scientist that studies amphibians and reptiles. The study of amphibians and reptiles is called herpetology.

Iris – the colored part of the eye, which controls the size of the opening that lets light into the eyeball.

Lens – the part of the eye just behind the iris that controls how light hits the retina.

Membrane – a thin layer of skin.

Nocturnal – having to do with night. Nocturnal animals do most of their activities at night, while spending the day quietly in sheltered places.

Olfactory – having to do with the sense of smell. The olfactory nerves transmit nerve signals to the brain.

Optic nerves – the nerves that connect the retina to the brain.

Photoreceptors – nerve cells that react to light by sending a signal to the brain.

Predator – an animal that kills and eats another animal. The animal that is eaten is the prey.

Pupil – the opening, controlled by the iris, that lets light into the eye. The pupil is the dark spot in the middle of the eye.

Retina – the light-sensitive layer of tissue at the back of the eyeball.

Slit sensilla – thin areas that look like openings in the exo-skeleton of spiders, which are important sensory organs.

Tympanum – the skin-covered disk in the ear that vibrates due to sound waves in the air and starts the hearing process.

BIBLIOGRAPHY

Barth, Friedrich G. *A Spider's World: Senses and Behavior.* Berlin: Springer, 2002.

Barth, Friedrich G. "A Spider's Tactile Hairs." Scholarpedia. November 3, 2015. http://www.scholarpedia.org/article/A_spider's_tactile_hairs.

Brown, David and Neil B. Carmony. *Gila Monster: Facts and Folklore of America's Aztec Lizard.* Salt Lake City, UT: University of Utah Press, 1999.

Brown, Tom. *The Tracker: The Story of Tom Brown, Jr. as Told to William Jon Watkins.* New York: Berkley Books, 1985.

Cerveny, Jaroslav. "Directional Preference May Enhance Hunting Accuracy in Foraging Foxes." Biology Letters. January 12, 2011. http://rsbl.royalsocietypublishing.org/content/7/3/355.

Elliot, Lang. *A Guide to Night Sounds.* Mechanicsburg, PA: Stackpole Books, 2004.

Evans, Charles. *Vomeronasal Chemoreception in Vertebrates: A Study of the Second Nose.* London, UK: Imperial College Press, 2003.

Foltán, René, and Jiří Šedý. "Behavioral Changes of Patients after Orthognathic Surgery Develop on the Basis of the Loss of Vomeronasal Organ: An Hypothesis." *Head & Face Medicine.* January 22, 2009. https://www.ncbi.nlm.nih.gov/pmc/articles/PMC2653472/.

Gibbs, James P. and Breisch, Alvin R. *The Amphibians and Reptiles of New York State: Identification, Natural History, and Conservation.* New York: Oxford University Press, 2007.

Hand, Eric. "The Body's Hidden Compass—What Is It, and How Does It Work?" Science Magazine. June 23, 2016. http://www.sciencemag.org/news/2016/06/body-s-hidden-compass-what-it-and-how-does-it-work.

Hart, Stephen. "Frog Calls." The Animal Communication Project. 2015. http://acp.eugraph.com/frogs/.

Heinrich, Bernd. *Winter World: The Ingenuity of Animal Survival.* New York: HarperCollins Publishers, 2003.

Hewitt, David G. *Biology and Management of White-tailed Deer.* Boca Raton, FL: CRC Press, 2011.

Hsu, Jeremy. "Cows Have Strange Sixth Sense." *LiveScience.* August 25, 2008. http://www.livescience.com/5083-cows-strange-sixth-sense.html.

Keller, Helen. *The World I Live In.* New York: The Century Co., 1908.

Long, Kim. *Frogs: A Wildlife Handbook.* Boulder, CO: Johnson Books, 1999.

Lynch, Wayne. *Owls of the United States and Canada: A Complete Guide to Their Biology and Behavior.* Baltimore, MD: Johns Hopkins University Press. 2007.

Reid, Catherine. *Coyote: Seeking the Hunter in Our Midst.* New York: Houghton Mifflin Co., 2004.

Shuker, Karl. *The Hidden Powers of Animals.* London, UK: Marshall Editions, 2001.

Solov'yov, Ilia, and Klaus Schulten. "Cryptochrome and Magnetic Sensing." Cryptochrome and Magnetic Sensing. January 23, 2014. http://www.ks.uiuc.edu/Research/cryptochrome/.

Yong, Ed. "Foxes Use the Earth's Magnetic Field as a Targeting System." Discover: Science for the Curious. 2011. http://blogs.discovermagazine.com/notrocketscience/2011/01/11/foxes-use-the-earths-magnetic-field-as-a-targeting-system/#.V_Jy_IWcFjo.